THE BOOK OF
GODS AND
DEVILS

WITHDRAWN

OTHER BOOKS BY CHARLES SIMIC

THE BOOK OF
GODS AND DEVILS

CHARLES SIMIC

Harcourt Brace Jovanovich, Publishers

San Diego   New York   London

Requests for permission to make copies of any part of the work
should be mailed to: Permissions Department,
Harcourt Brace Jovanovich, Publishers, Orlando, Florida 32887.

Some of these poems first appeared, often in different versions,
in the following magazines, to whose editors a grateful
acknowledgment is made: *Antaeus, Field, The Georgia
Review, The Gettysburg Review, Grand Street, The Ontario Review,
The Paris Review, Ploughshares, Poetry, The Poetry Miscellany,
The Southwest Review, Sulfur, The Western Humanities Review,
Witness.*

Library of Congress Cataloging-in-Publication Data
Simic, Charles, 1938–
     The book of Gods and devils : poems / Charles Simic. — 1st ed.
     p.   cm.
     ISBN 0-15-113455-3 — ISBN 0-15-613546-9 (pbk.)
     I. Title.
   PS3569.I4725B6   1990
   811'.54—dc20   90-4297

Designed by Trina Stahl
Printed in the United States of America
First edition
A B C D E

FOR HELEN

CONTENTS

PART ONE

PART TWO

PART THREE

PART ONE

THE LITTLE PINS OF MEMORY

There was a child's Sunday suit
Pinned to a tailor's dummy
In a dusty store window.
The store looked closed for years.

I lost my way there once
In a Sunday kind of quiet,
Sunday kind of afternoon light
On a street of red-brick tenements.

How do you like that?
I said to no one.
How do you like that?
I said it again today upon waking.

That street went on forever
And all along I could feel the pins
In my back, prickling
The dark and heavy cloth.

ST. THOMAS AQUINAS

I left parts of myself everywhere
The way absent-minded people leave
Gloves and umbrellas
Whose colors are sad from dispensing so much bad luck.

I was on a park bench asleep.
It was like the Art of Ancient Egypt.
I didn't wish to bestir myself.
I made my long shadow take the evening train.

"We give death to a child when we give it a doll,"
Said the woman who had read Djuna Barnes.
We whispered all night. She had traveled
      to darkest Africa.
She had many stories to tell about the jungle.

I was already in New York looking for work.
It was raining as in the days of Noah.
I stood in many doorways of that great city.
Once I asked a man in a tuxedo for a cigarette.
He gave me a frightened look and stepped out
      into the rain.

Since "man naturally desires happiness,"
According to St. Thomas Aquinas,
Who gave irrefutable proof of God's existence
      and purpose,
I loaded trucks in the Garment Center.

Me and a black man stole a woman's red dress.
It was of silk; it shimmered.

Upon a gloomy night with all our loving ardors on fire,
We carried it down the long empty avenue,
Each holding one sleeve.
The heat was intolerable causing many terrifying
    human faces
To come out of hiding.

In the Public Library Reading Room
There was a single ceiling fan barely turning.
I had the travels of Herman Melville to serve me as a
    pillow.
I was on a ghost ship with its sails fully raised.
I could see no land anywhere.
The sea and its monsters could not cool me.

I followed a saintly-looking nurse into a doctor's office.
We edged past people with eyes and ears bandaged.
"I am a medieval philosopher in exile,"
I explained to my landlady that night.
And, truly, I no longer looked like myself.
I wore glasses with a nasty spider crack over one eye.

I stayed in the movies all day long.
A woman on the screen walked through a bombed city
Again and again. She wore army boots.
Her legs were long and bare. It was cold
    wherever she was.

She had her back turned to me, but I was
    in love with her.
I expected to find wartime Europe at the exit.

It wasn't even snowing! Everyone I met
Wore a part of my destiny like a carnival mask.
"I'm Bartleby the Scrivener," I told the Italian waiter.
"Me, too," he replied.
And I could see nothing but overflowing ashtrays
The human-faced flies were busy examining.

A LETTER

Dear philosophers, I get sad when I think.
Is it the same with you?
Just as I'm about to sink my teeth into the noumenon,
Some old girlfriend comes to distract me.
"She's not even alive!" I yell to the skies.

The wintry light made me go that way.
I saw beds covered with identical gray blankets.
I saw grim-looking men holding a naked woman
While they hosed her with cold water.
Was that to calm her nerves, or was it punishment?

I went to visit my friend Bob who said to me:
"We reach the real by overcoming the
    seduction of images."
I was overjoyed, until I realized
Such abstinence will never be possible for me.
I caught myself looking out the window.

Bob's father was taking their dog for a walk.
He moved with pain; the dog waited for him.
There was no one else in the park,
Only bare trees with an infinity of tragic shapes
To make thinking difficult.

FACTORY

The machines were gone, and so were those
    who worked them.
A single high-backed chair stood like a throne
In all that empty space.
I was on the floor making myself comfortable
For a long night of little sleep and much thinking.

An empty bird cage hung from a steam pipe.
In it I kept an apple and a small paring knife.
I placed newspapers all around me on the floor
So I could jump at the slightest rustle.
It was like the scratching of a pen,
The silence of the night writing in its diary.

Of rats who came to pay me a visit
I had the highest opinion.
They'd stand on two feet
As if about to make a polite request
On a matter of great importance.

Many other strange things came to pass.
Once a naked woman climbed on the chair
To reach the apple in the cage.
I was on the floor watching her go on tiptoe,
Her hand fluttering in the cage like a bird.

On other days, the sun peeked through dusty
    windowpanes
To see what time it was. But there was no clock,

Only the knife in the cage, glinting like a mirror,
And the chair in the far corner
Where someone once sat facing the brick wall.

SHELLEY

for M. Follain

Poet of the dead leaves driven like ghosts,
Driven like pestilence-stricken multitudes,
I read you first
One rainy evening in New York City,

In my atrocious Slavic accent,
Saying the mellifluous verses
From a battered, much-stained volume
I had bought earlier that day
In a second-hand bookstore on Fourth Avenue
Run by an initiate of the occult masters.

The little money I had being almost spent,
I walked the streets my nose in the book.
I sat in a dingy coffee shop
With last summer's dead flies on the table.
The owner was an ex-sailor
Who had grown a huge hump on his back
While watching the rain, the empty street.
He was glad to have me sit and read.
He'd refill my cup with a liquid dark as river Styx.

Shelley spoke of a mad, blind, dying king;
Of rulers who neither see, nor feel, nor know;
Of graves from which a glorious Phantom may
Burst to illumine our tempestuous day.

I too felt like a glorious phantom
Going to have my dinner
In a Chinese restaurant I knew so well.
It had a three-fingered waiter
Who'd bring my soup and rice each night
Without ever saying a word.

I never saw anyone else there.
The kitchen was separated by a curtain
Of glass beads which clicked faintly
Whenever the front door opened.
The front door opened that evening
To admit a pale little girl with glasses.

The poet spoke of the everlasting universe
Of things . . . of gleams of a remoter world
Which visit the soul in sleep . . .
Of a desert peopled by storms alone . . .

The streets were strewn with broken umbrellas
Which looked like funereal kites
This little Chinese girl might have made.
The bars on MacDougal Street were emptying.
There had been a fist fight.
A man leaned against a lamp post arms extended
    as if crucified,
The rain washing the blood off his face.

In a dimly lit side street,
Where the sidewalk shone like a ballroom mirror
At closing time—

A well-dressed man without any shoes
Asked me for money.
His eyes shone, he looked triumphant
Like a fencing master
Who had just struck a mortal blow.

How strange it all was . . . The world's raffle
That dark October night . . .
The yellowed volume of poetry
With its Splendors and Glooms
Which I studied by the light of storefronts:
Drugstores and barbershops,
Afraid of my small windowless room
Cold as a tomb of an infant emperor.

THE DEVILS

You were a "victim of semiromantic anarchism
In its most irrational form."
I was "ill at ease in an ambiguous world

Deserted by Providence." We drank gin
And made love in the afternoon. The neighbors'
TV's were tuned to soap operas.

The unhappy couples spoke little.
There were interminable pauses.
Soft organ music. Someone coughing.

"It's like Strindberg's *Dream Play*," you said.
"What is?" I asked and got no reply.
I was watching a spider on the ceiling.

It was the kind St. Veronica ate in her martyrdom.
"That woman subsisted on spiders only,"
I told the janitor when he came to fix the faucet.

He wore dirty overalls and a derby hat.
Once he had been an inmate of a notorious
     state institution.
"I'm no longer Jesus," he informed us happily.

He believed only in devils now.
"This building is full of them," he confided.
One could see their horns and tails

If one caught them in their baths.
"He's got Dark Ages on his brain," you said.
"Who does?" I asked and got no reply.

The spider had the beginnings of a web
Over our heads. The world was quiet
Except when one of us took a sip of gin.

CREPUSCULE WITH NELLIE

for Ira

Monk at the Five Spot
    late one night.
Ruby my Dear, Epistrophy.
    The place nearly empty
Because of the cold spell.
One beautiful black transvestite
    alone up front,
Sipping his drink demurely.

The music Pythagorean,
    one note at a time
Connecting the heavenly spheres,
While I leaned against the bar
    surveying the premises
Through cigarette smoke.

All of a sudden, a clear sense
    of a memorable occasion . . .
The joy of it, the delicious melancholy . . .
This very strange man bent over the piano
    shaking his head, humming . . .

Misterioso.

Then it was all over, thank you!
Chairs being stacked up on tables,
    their legs up.

The prospect of the freeze outside,
    the long walk home,
Making one procrastinatory.

Who said Americans don't have history,
    only endless nostalgia?
And where the hell was Nellie?

THE BIG MACHINE

The insides of the machine at night
Like a garden of carnivorous plants.
There goes the mad doctor in short pants
Wielding a butterfly net.

Hairpins, shaving mirrors, blown-up condoms
With spikes, or could they be levers,
Pulleys, dangling counterweights
Enacting their shadow-farces and tragedies?

Is it a lady's dainty slipper
They're raising or lowering,
Or the ghost of the machine
Riding an empty swing?

The Monster who can't tell
Plugs himself into an electric outlet
And gathers a spray
Of pig-iron immortelles.

TWO DOGS

for Charles and Holly

An old dog afraid of his own shadow
In some Southern town.
The story told me by a woman going blind,
One fine summer evening
As shadows were creeping
Out of the New Hampshire woods,
A long street with just a worried dog
And a couple of dusty chickens,
And all that sun beating down
In that nameless Southern town.

It made me remember the Germans marching
Past our house in 1944.
The way everybody stood on the sidewalk
Watching them out of the corner of the eye,
The earth trembling, death going by . . .
A little white dog ran into the street
And got entangled with the soldiers' feet.
A kick made him fly as if he had wings.
That's what I keep seeing!
Night coming down. A dog with wings.

LE BEAU MONDE

A man got up to talk about Marcel Proust,
"The great French writer,"
From a soapbox famous for its speeches
About crooked bosses and the working poor.

I swear it (Tony Russo is my witness).
It was late one night, the crowd was thinning,
But then they all came back
To see what his mumbling was all about.

He looked like a dishwasher
From one of the dives on Avenue B.
He chewed his nails as he spoke.
He said this and that in what must've been French.

Everybody perked up, even the winos.
The tough guys stopped flexing their muscles.
It was like being in church
When the High Mass was said in Latin.

Nobody had a clue, but it made you feel good.
When it was over, he just walked away,
Long-legged and in a big hurry.
The rest of us taking our time to disperse.

EVENING TALK

Everything you didn't understand
Made you what you are. Strangers
Whose eye you caught on the street
Studying you. Perhaps they were the all-seeing
Illuminati? They knew what you didn't,
And left you troubled like a strange dream.

Not even the light stayed the same.
Where did all that hard glare come from?
And the scent, as if mythical beings
Were being groomed and fed stalks of hay
On these roofs drifting among the evening clouds.

You didn't understand a thing!
You loved the crowds at the end of the day
That brought you so many mysteries.
There was always someone you were meant to meet
Who for some reason wasn't waiting.
Or perhaps they were? But not here, friend.

You should have crossed the street
And followed that obviously demented woman
With the long streak of blood-red hair
Which the sky took up like a distant cry.

THE BETROTHAL

I found a key
In the street, someone's
House key
Lying there, glinting,

Long ago; the one
Who lost it
Is not going to remember it
Tonight, as I do.

It was a huge city
Of many dark windows,
Columns and domes.
I stood there thinking.

The street ahead of me
Shadowy, full of peril
Now that I held
The key. One or two

Late strollers
Unhurried and grave
In view. The sky above them
Of an unearthly clarity.

Eternity jealous
Of the present moment,
It occurred to me!
And then the moment was over.

FRIGHTENING TOYS

History practicing its scissor-clips
In the dark,
So everything comes out in the end
Missing an arm or a leg.

Still, if that's all you've got
To play with today . . .
This doll at least had a head,
And its lips were red!

Frame houses like grim exhibits
Lining the empty street
Where a little girl sat on the steps
In a flowered nightgown, talking to it.

It looked like a serious matter,
Even the rain wanted to hear about it,
So it fell on her eyelashes,
And made them glisten.

THE NORTH

The ancients knew the sorrows of exile:
If you weren't hanged, they'd pack you off
To the far ends of the Earth,
To go on grumbling, writing endless petitions
That would never reach the Emperor.

The North always the place of punishment:
Unforgiving cold, rags on your back,
And the company of a few sullen barbarians
At day's end when the wind parts the clouds
And the stars seem to be mocking.

Every few years a garbled message from home.
Memory paying a call in the wee hours:
A mother's face; the company of merry friends
At the long table in the garden;
Their wives baring their throats in the
    afternoon heat . . .

"The sages suffered, too, exiled from truth,"
That's what you tell yourself . . .
Not many are meant to retrace their steps
And behold the splendors of the capital
Even more seductive than when you knew them.

The North always the place of punishment.
Deep snow. Blue-veined trees and bushes
Rising against the pink-colored morning sky . . .
So that briefly, in that one spell,
Your heartache hushes at the beauty of it.

PART TWO

MARCHING MUSIC

Our history is both tragic and comic.
Beat the big drum, fellows!
Horsemen of the Apocalypse,
What fun it was to pull your horses' tails!
The earth trembled.

Mighty towers collapsed.
Towers of chairs still warm
With backsides of kings and queens,
Towers of pisspots, too,
Where our philosophers sat thinking.

We stood with our mouths open
Admiring the fashionable black hoods
The horses and the coachmen wore
As they hauled off the trash to the infinite.

Beat the big drum, fellows!
On the Square of Eternal Happiness
A woman ran by shrieking,
Hugging a blood-stained shirt.

A BIT OF MUMMERY

for Fanny Howe

In the corner of your eye
Where death cools his heels,
A skit, a dumb show
That took a wink to perform,
That took an eternity!

Your mother and father
With a ventriloquist's dummy
(That was you
With cheeks painted red),

Approaching a couple of soldiers.
(They are armed.)
The woman is pleading. The dummy
Sits in your father's arms
Grinning from ear to ear.

It's a day like today
Thirty years ago,
So bright, so sunny,
Everybody has to squint.

THE BIG WAR

We played war during the war,
Margaret. Toy soldiers were in big demand,
The kind made from clay.
The lead ones they melted into bullets, I suppose.

You never saw anything as beautiful
As those clay regiments! I used to lie on the floor
For hours staring them in the eye.
I remember them staring back at me in wonder.

How strange they must have felt
Standing stiffly at attention
Before a large, incomprehending creature
With a moustache made of milk.

In time they broke, or I broke them on purpose.
There was wire inside their limbs,
Inside their chests, but nothing in the heads!
Margaret, I made sure.

Nothing at all in the heads . . .
Just an arm, now and then, an officer's arm,
Wielding a saber from a crack
In my deaf grandmother's kitchen floor.

BREAD

Stale loaf
Left for us
On a plate

Dinnertime
Our clever sister
Tucked it into a sock
Teethmarks intact

Tied a red ribbon
Round its neck
To indicate which is the head
Which is the heart

Rocked the babe
Who kept crying
For a brother
The dearest one

No bigger than
That ball of lint
Under the high
And empty bed

DEATH, THE PHILOSOPHER

He gives excellent advice by example.
"See!" he says. "See that?"
And he doesn't have to open his mouth
To tell you what.
You can trust his vast experience.
Still, there's no huff in him.
Once he had a most unfortunate passion.
It came to an end.
He loved the way the summer dusk fell.
He wanted to have it falling forever.
It was not possible.
That was the big secret.
It's dreadful when things get as bad as that—
But then they don't!
He got the point, and so, one day,
Miraculously lucid, you, too, came to ask
About the strangeness of it all.
Charles, you said,
How strange you should be here at all!

FIRST THING IN THE MORNING

To find a bit of thread
But twisted
In a peculiar way
And fallen
In an unlikely place

A black thread
Before the mystery
Of a closed door
The greater mystery
Of the four bare walls

And catch oneself thinking
Do I know anyone
Who wears such dark garments
Worn to threads
First thing in the morning?

THE WHITE ROOM

The obvious is difficult
To prove. Many prefer
The hidden. I did, too.
I listened to the trees.

They had a secret
Which they were about to
Make known to me,
And then didn't.

Summer came. Each tree
On my street had its own
Scheherazade. My nights
Were a part of their wild

Story-telling. We were
Entering dark houses,
More and more dark houses
Hushed and abandoned.

There was someone with eyes closed
On the upper floors.
The thought of it, and the wonder,
Kept me sleepless.

The truth is bald and cold,
Said the woman
Who always wore white.
She didn't leave her room much.

The sun pointed to one or two
Things that had survived
The long night intact,
The simplest things,

Difficult in their obviousness.
They made no noise.
It was the kind of day
People describe as "perfect."

Gods disguising themselves
As black hairpins? A hand-mirror?
A comb with a tooth missing?
No! That wasn't it.

Just things as they are,
Unblinking, lying mute
In that bright light,
And the trees waiting for the night.

BEYOND APPEARANCES

A sort of vast, undetected conspiracy
In which even the leaves participate.
When they rustle, when they deign to fall,
It's because they've been told to.

There had to be many clandestine meetings
To which the wind and its cohorts were invited.
They gave the secret password,
Something above suspicion, like "It's morning."

There's a strange man walking past our house.
If he's a hunter, why is he wearing black?
Before we can decide, he has vanished,
And the dog didn't even bother to lift his head.

A cold day breaking over the fields . . .
At least, there should've been a cloud of breath
Preceding him . . . plus one or two other things
We still can't bring ourselves to mention.

THE MEANING

Hidden like that small boy
They couldn't find
The day they played hide-and-seek
In a park full of dead trees.

We give up! they yelled.

It was getting dark.
They had to summon his mother
To order him to come out.
First she threatened him,
Then she was frightened.

At long last they heard a twig
Snap behind their backs,
And there it was!
The stone dwarf, the angel in the fountain.

CELESTIAL OVERSEERS

Do they count my steps meticulously?
Have they reached a figure
Of many zeros separated by commas?
Could I have walked to the nearest star already?

Recall for me, please,
One of my first steps.
I want the suit I was wearing that day pressed.
I want my mother to hold my hand tightly.

That must be our grandmother there
In the open coffin. Her hands are chapped
From scrubbing so much
The floor we walk on in black shoes.

The three little steps I took then
So that I might be lifted up to kiss her,
And the three equally tiny ones to withdraw . . .
Do they still resound at ever-receding magnitudes?

Could this large dog sitting sphinxlike
By the gray Atlantic shore
Still hear my new shoes squeaking
On the other side of the world?

WINTER SUNSET

Such skies came to worry men
On the eve of great battles:
Clouds soaked in blood of the dying day
That made the horses restless,

So the soothsayers were summoned
But kept their mouths shut
About the meaning of it,
Even when shown the naked sword.

The gloomy heavens made gloomier
By the shadow play of unknown tribes
And their heroes on the run.
The white church tower of the First Congregational

Clutching its bird-shaped weathervane
Against it all, but the village deserted.
Not a soul in sight. The people indoors
Afraid to get up and turn on the lights.

Some young farm woman, dress unbuttoned,
A small child on her knees,
Its head turning away from her full breast . . .
Eyes full of the sky's terror and luster.

A WORD

Said by a child who doesn't know
The meaning of it. The neighbors
Coming to hear all about it,
But the door's locked. No one at home.

It's such a nice warm day
To be lost in a strange city.
The map of ancient Rome in your pocket,
Or is it Jerusalem?

"Please make him stop," she says.
We can only see her blood-red fingernails
Drying on the windowsill.
The one she's speaking to remains silent.

He's just an idea, anyway,
Sulking in some back room
With a somber view of its own. The child
Who cannot be put into words.

MRS. DIGBY'S PICTURE ALBUM

A child shrieks with terror.
The men laugh.
The apple trees are in blossom.
Smoke trails the evening train.

No sheep on the green meadow.
No bones in the old graveyard.

Abruptly a bird takes off.
A suitcase sits by the railroad tracks.

Mrs. Digby's watch has no hands,
But it keeps running.

The river is cold and full of dark thoughts.
The dog's eyes are large and childlike.

Mrs. Digby clutches a Bible to her bosom.

In her hat the feather of a bird
That lives in a tiger's cage.

*

Where the river lay shadowy
By the weeping willows,
They bathed in the long twilight.
Huge women,
Wet hair streaming down their faces.

A child, too, that wandered off,
Never to be found again.
Don't you hear it crying still?
Death's new ribbon in its hair.

The same dark woods
Where the young witch
Used to run over the snow
In red slippers.

Mrs. Digby turning on the table lamp
For her moth to come
Fluttering out of the trees,

The whitest moth you'll ever see.

*

Beloved Amy, Ada, Amelia, Amanda . . .

Village of endless disappointments.
A long starless night on its way.

The howl of the dog afraid of the dark,
And the wind like a dragon
On a tin box of Chinese tea.

The river hushed,
Its other bank already blurred
Like their voices once . . .

Their high laughter
Muffled by the leaves.

Mrs. Digby's one-armed scarecrow
In the tall backyard weeds
Pointing to the spot.

THE PIECES OF THE CLOCK LIE SCATTERED

So, hurry up!
The evening's coming.
The grown-ups are on the way.
There'll be hell to pay.

You forgot about time
While you sought its secret
In the slippery wheels,
Some of which had teeth.

You meant to enthrall
The girl across the hall.
She drew so near,
Her breast brushed your ear.

She ought to have gone home,
But you kept telling her
You'll have it together again
And ticking in no time.

Instead, you're under the table
Together, searching the floor.
Your hands are trembling,
And there's a key in the door.

THE PRONOUN

Many people saying
It

Many others answering
To *it*
Without identifying it further

Some animal or thing

Very thoughtful of them
I'm sure
With the world so full of unknowns
Crowding around us

Pit pit pit
Is how the wood thrush put *it*

Which is why
We are gathered here this evening
In the absence of
In the terrifying presence of

The pale moon early risen
The darkening earth
Trees wearing their fright wigs

A huge man casting a shadow
Of a small child
A dog with a soul by his side

Waiting for *it*

HEIGHTS OF FOLLY

O crows circling over my head and cawing!
I admit to being, at times,
Suddenly, and without the slightest warning,
Exceedingly happy,

On a morning otherwise sunless,
Strolling arm in arm
Past some gallows-shaped trees
With my dear Helen,
Who is also a strange bird.

A feeling of being summoned
Urgently, but by a most gracious invitation
To breakfast on slices of watermelon
In the company of naked gods and goddesses
On a patch of last night's snow.

THE IMMORTAL

You're shivering, O my memory.
You went out early and without a coat
To visit your old schoolmasters,
The cruel schoolmasters and their pet monkeys.
You took a wrong turn somewhere.
You met an army of gray days,
A ghost army of years on the march.
It was the bread they fed you,
The kind it takes a lifetime to chew.

You found yourself again on that street
Inside that small, rented room
With its single dusty window.
Outside it was snowing quietly,
Snowing and snowing for days on end.
You were ill and in bed.
Everyone else had gone to work.
The blind old woman next door,
Whose sighs and heavy steps you'd welcome now,
Had died mysteriously in the summer.

You had your own heartbeat to attend to.
You were perfectly alone and anonymous.
It would have taken months for anyone
To begin to miss you. The chill
Made you pull the covers up to your chin.

You remembered the lost arctic voyagers,
The evening snow erasing their footprints.

You had no money and no job.
Both of your lungs were hurting; still,
You had no intention of lifting a finger
To help yourself. You were immortal!

Outside, the same dark snowflake
Seemed to be falling over and over again.
You studied the cracked walls,
The maplike water stain on the ceiling,
Trying to fix in your mind its cities and rivers.

Time had stopped at dusk.
You were shivering at the thought
Of such great happiness.

PART THREE

AT THE CORNER

The fat sisters
Kept a candy store
Dim and narrow
With dusty jars
Of jaw-breaking candy.

We stayed thin, stayed
Glum, chewing gum
While staring at the floor,
The shoes of many strangers
Rushing in and out,

Making the papers outside
Flutter audibly
Under the lead weights,
Their headlines
Screaming in and out of view.

WITH EYES VEILED

First they dream about it,
Then they go looking for it.
The cities are full of figments.
Some even carry parcels.

Trust me. It's not there.
Perhaps in the opposite direction,
On some street you took by chance
Having grown tired of the search.

A dusty storefront waits for you
Full of religious paraphernalia
Made by the blind. The store
Padlocked. Night falling.

The blue and gold Madonna in the window
Smiles with her secret knowledge.
Exotic rings on her fat fingers.
A black stain where her child used to be.

CHILDHOOD STORY

The streets were wider, the houses bigger.
A red-haired giantess with huge breasts
Took you into her bed. There you heard again
The story of the king's youngest daughter.

The ball she played with rolled into a pond
Full of dead leaves. It stayed there.
You already knew you'd find it someday.
You'd enter a quiet, sun-burnished room,

And there'd be that ball on the table . . .
It was black from spending so much time
In other people's dreams. You told no one about it.
The earth is a ball, you heard your father say.

He sat in a lion-footed chair with a sheet over his head
As if waiting for movers. The roads out of town
Were packed with sleepwalkers dressed as soldiers.
They must not be wakened, you were warned.

Was it true that they always drew the victim's name
Out of a hat? That there were forbidden rooms
Only bad children and mad housewives entered?
That the ball in the story used to be golden?

THE WORLD

As if I were a big old shade tree
On a side street with a small café.
Neon beer sign with the word "cold" shining in it.
Summer dusk.

The solitary customer, who looks like my father,
Is bent over a book with small print
Oblivious of the young waiter
Who is about to serve him a cup of black coffee.

I have an incalculable number of leaves
Not one of which is moving.
It's because we are enchanted, I think.
We don't have a care in the world.

WEATHER OF THE SOUL

It's raining, it's pouring,
And your heart is very sad,
But you're not about to confess it.

Enough rain to make the river overflow,
The nuns at the hospital
To load their mad patients in a big rowboat.

If it eases a little, send the boy next door
For beer. Let him bring cigars, too,
Under your big black umbrella.

His mother is beautiful when she smiles,
But she rarely does,
Even when she breast-feeds the baby.

You can't say "wild desire,"
And it's silly to say "I've been spooked
By the way she thinks with her eyes,"

Thinks and thinks,
While on the roof the rain makes the sound
Of old-fashioned petticoats.

WHOSE EYES TO CATCH,
WHOSE EYES TO AVOID

She has just walked by,
The one who will deign to sit
At the reading of my sentence
With a young babe in her arms.

It's the child's father they'll be watching
Adjust the noose around my neck.
They'll know him by his uncommonly large hands,
Despite the black hood.

Today she carried only her purse
And was coatless even with the weather so cold,
Bare-legged and in such a short skirt,
As she threw me a passing glance . . .

And the huge hands of her husband near her,
Which I examined closely for drops of blood,
But found them instead to be spotless
With many small blond hairs the sunlight
    had turned gold.

THE GODS

The statues of Greek gods
In the storage room of the art school
Where I led Pamela by the hand,
Or was it she who led me?
Nibbled my ear, while I raised her skirt.

Identical Apollos held identical
Empty hands. Poor imitations,
I thought. They belong in a window
Of a store going out of business
On a street dark and desolate.

That's because my eyes were closed
Long before they were open again.
It was night. There was still light,
Enough to tell their nakedness from ours,
But I couldn't figure where it came from,
And how long it meant to stay.

CABBAGE

She was about to chop the head
In half,
But I made her reconsider
By telling her:
"Cabbage symbolizes mysterious love."

Or so said one Charles Fourier,
Who said many other strange and wonderful things,
So that people called him mad behind his back,

Whereupon I kissed the back of her neck
Ever so gently,

Whereupon she cut the cabbage in two
With a single stroke of her knife.

THE INITIATE

St. John of the Cross wore dark glasses
As he passed me on the street.
St. Theresa of Avila, beautiful and grave,
Turned her back on me.

"Soulmate," they shouted. "It's high time."

I was a blind child, a wind-up toy.
I was one of death's juggling red balls
On a certain street corner
Where they peddle things out of suitcases.

The city like a huge cinema
With lights dimmed.
The performance already started.

So many blurred faces in a complicated plot.

The great secret which kept eluding me:
    knowing who I am . . .

The Redeemer and the Virgin,
Their eyes wide open in the empty church
Where the killer came to hide himself . . .

The new snow on the sidewalk bore footprints
That could have been made by bare feet.
Some unknown penitent guiding me.

In truth, I didn't know where I was going.
My feet were frozen,
My stomach growled.

Four young hoods blocking my way.
Three deadpan, one smiling crazily.

I let them have my black raincoat.

Thinking constantly of the Divine Love and
    the Absolute had disfigured me.
People mistook me for someone else.
I heard voices after me calling out unknown names.

"I'm searching for someone to sell my soul to,"
The drunk who followed me whispered,
While appraising me from head to foot.

At the address I had been given,
The building had large X's over its windows.
I knocked but no one came to open.
By and by a black girl joined me on the steps.
She banged at the door till her fist hurt.

Her name was Alma, a propitious sign.
She knew someone who solved life's riddles
In a voice of an ancient Sumerian queen.
We had a long talk about that
While shivering and stamping our wet feet.

It was necessary to stay calm, I explained,
Even with the earth trembling,
And to continue to watch oneself
As if one were a complete stranger.

Once in a hotel room in Chicago
I caught sight of a man in a shaving mirror
Who had my naked shoulders and face,
But whose eyes terrified me!

Two hard staring, all-knowing eyes!

Alma, the night, the cold, and the endless walking
Brought on a kind of ecstasy.
I went as if pursued, trying to warm myself.

There was the East River; there was the Hudson.
Their waters shone like oil in sanctuary lamps.

Something supreme was occurring
For which there will never be any words.
The sky was full of racing clouds and tall buildings,
Whirling and whirling silently.

In that whole city you could hear a pin drop.
Believe me,
I thought I heard a pin drop and I went looking for it.

PARADISE

In a neighborhood once called "Hell's-Kitchen"
Where a beggar claimed to be playing Nero's fiddle
While the city burned in mid-summer heat;
Where a lady barber who called herself Cleopatra
Wielded the scissors of fate over my head
Threatening to cut off my ears and nose;
Where a man and a woman went walking naked
In one of the dark side streets at dawn.

I must be dreaming, I told myself.
It was like meeting a couple of sphinxes.
I expected them to have wings, bodies of lions:
Him with his wildly tattooed chest;
Her with her huge, dangling breasts.

It happened so quickly, and so long ago!

You know that time just before the day breaks
When one yearns to lie down on cool sheets
In a room with shades drawn?
The hour when the beautiful suicides
Lying side by side in the morgue
Get up and walk out into the first light.

The curtains of cheap hotels flying out of windows
Like sea gulls, but everything else quiet . . .
Steam rising out of the subway gratings . . .
Bodies glistening with sweat . . .
Madness, and you might even say, paradise!

BABYLON

Every time I prayed
The universe got bigger,
And I got smaller.

My wife almost stepped on me.
I saw her huge legs
Rising to dizzying heights.
The hair between them
Glistened like a god's beard.
She looked Babylonian.

"I'm getting smaller every minute,"
I yelled, but she could not hear me
Among the winged lions and ziggurats,
The mad astrologers of her painted eyes.

IN THE LIBRARY

for Octavio

There's a book called
"A Dictionary of Angels."
No one has opened it in fifty years,
I know, because when I did,
The covers creaked, the pages
Crumbled. There I discovered

The angels were once as plentiful
As species of flies.
The sky at dusk
Used to be thick with them.
You had to wave both arms
Just to keep them away.

Now the sun is shining
Through the tall windows.
The library is a quiet place.
Angels and gods huddled
In dark unopened books.
The great secret lies
On some shelf Miss Jones
Passes every day on her rounds.

She's very tall, so she keeps
Her head tipped as if listening.
The books are whispering.
I hear nothing, but she does.

THE WINDOW

Serious-looking
Nearsighted old woman
Cutting her nails
In a shadowy room

Lit by a single lamp
At the long table
Which also holds a vase
Of fake blood-red roses

The scissors big and loud
At each clip
Quarter-moons falling
Yellow bird-claws

One thinks of love potions
Carefully concocted
Unrequited passion from which
Great hatred is born

And now the pleasure
Of these long nails
Cut down
To where flesh is raw

THE WAIL

As if there were nothing to live for . . .
As if there were . . . nothing.
In the fading light, our mother
Sat sewing with her head bowed.

Did her hand tremble? By the first faint
Hint of night coming, how all lay
Still, except for the memory of that voice:
Him whom the wild life hurried away . . .

Long stretches of silence in between.
Clock talking to a clock.
Dogs lying on their paws with ears cocked.
You and me afraid to breathe.

Finally, she went to peek. Someone covered
With a newspaper on the sidewalk.
Otherwise, no one about. The street empty.
The sky full of gypsy clouds.

THE BOOK OF MAGIC

It called for the evening to come,
The table to be spread with white cloth.
Two apples, two knives to be set out,
And a single glass of red wine.
It called for him to be asleep in bed,
For two unknown women to enter,
To eat the apples, drink the wine,
And decide which one will stay with him.

But now it was still a little early.
He was the one lying in bed
Staring at the darkening ceiling.
The evening will never come.
The trees will darken and grow still,
But the sky will keep its pale color,
And so will the tablecloth.

And the evening will never come.
He will lie there with the window open
Listening for their footsteps.
He will tell himself how the women
Have taken off their high-heeled shoes.
They're coming arm in arm
With the evening and its shadows.

If even now he cannot hear them,
If everything remains just as it was,
It's because they're taking care not to be seen
Coming to stay with him,
The dark hours, the unknown women.

THE SCARECROW

God's refuted but the devil's not.

This year's tomatoes are something to see.
Bite into them, Martha,
As you would into a ripe apple.
After each bite add a little salt.

If the juices run down your chin
Onto your bare breasts,
Bend over the kitchen sink.

From there you can see your husband
Come to a dead stop in the empty field
Before one of his bleakest thoughts
Spreading its arms like a scarecrow.

WINDY EVENING

This old world needs propping up
When it gets this cold and windy.
The cleverly painted sets,
Oh, they're shaking badly!
They're about to come down.

There'll be nothing but infinite space then.
The silence supreme. Almighty silence.
Egyptian sky. Stars like torches
Of grave robbers entering the crypts of the kings.
Even the wind pausing, waiting to see.

Better grab hold of that tree, Lucille.
Its shape crazed, terror-stricken.
I'll hold the barn.
The chickens in it uneasy.
Smart chickens, rickety world.

FOURTEENTH STREET POEM

for Drena

The bag lady who shouted
She was Venus,
The Goddess of Love!
Had two front teeth missing.

It was a long block
Favored by doomsday prophets,
Blind street musicians,
Dogs licking their padlocks.

Photographs of missing children
Watched us meet and separate:
Me with a deep bow, her
With a finger on her lips
Making it "our" secret.